PRESENTS

Linger
Flash Fiction, Poetry, and Drama

Catherine D'Agostino

Iron Pelican
PUBLICATIONS

www.ironpelicanpublications.com

Iron Pelican Publications, LLC
24 Woodward Drive
Fredonia, NY 14063

First edition

ISBN: 979-8-9880009-6-9

Published by Iron Pelican Publications
in the United States of America

DEDICATION

A heartfelt thank you to the Friends of Chautauqua Writers' Center, a division of the Literary Arts Center at Chautauqua Institution, for supporting the craft of writing prose and poetry, especially Janay Cosner and Fred Zirm.

Table of Contents

Flash Fiction: 100-Word Stories

Public displays of affection at the Airbnb

The online advertisement described it as a romantic getaway with swaying palm trees, cushioned loungers, a swim-up tiki bar. I watched your eyes evaluate the concrete barrier wall lined with cracked barrels of browning leaves. I watched you peer into the deep end at the submerged wire chairs that had been blown in, who knows when. Your words were soft. "Where will I read my book?" And then you watched me, mystified, as I dove deep to drag up a metal chair and set it before you like a golden throne. "You can read it right here, love. Right here."

Your daily newspaper

All before sunrise, they are pressed, pounded, torn, and bound, then pushed out to wait on poorly lit street corners for paying customers to take them home. There, some are spread wide, flipped, cut, their smeared mascara leaving dark smudges on curious fingers. Others are ignored, sometimes left to suffocate under the weight of their predecessors. The ones spared this fate fare no better back at the office, where their edges are closely clipped to fit into marked envelopes lining long, cold metal drawers. In this morgue, they wait for salvation, but no one ever comes to identify their bodies.

When a narrow snow band swallows the sun

Armies of angry flakes pelt our windshield.

"Do you know your right and left?"

I formed the letter L with my left index finger and thumb.

My father nodded. "Stick your head out the window. Tell me how to steer, more right or left. Keep us on the road."

"I'm eight," I said.

His voice cracked. "I can't see ahead, and I can't stop. Please."

"What if I fall out?"

"I'll hold your ankles."

And that's how it went for miles.

Once in our driveway, I collapsed into my seat, welcoming my father's warm hands thumping my chest in victory.

Heart attack snow, it's called

In late November, when water vapor from the warm northeastern Great Lakes rises and clashes with cold sweeps of Canadian arctic air, a scientific phenomenon transforms those crystals into larger, denser frozen flakes in the upper atmosphere. In relentless droves, they dive-bomb highways, sidewalks, and roofs, thatching themselves into an unseen, heavy layer of wet super slush. From here, they select shovelers indiscriminately, regardless of age, gender, race, height, weight, prominence, or strength of will. A shovel's scrape on concrete releases their icy fingers to crawl up to the unsuspecting victim's chest for a tight squeeze that won't let go.

Never date a guy who just got a puppy

He needed someone to let out Bear at 6:30 each evening,
Monday to Friday, so Matt told Lillie he loved her. He knew
she had been waiting for his proclamation for three months
now, but didn't officially mumble the words until Thursday,
after the foreman told him he was being moved to second shift
for the summer. Matt had hoped Lillie would simply say it back
so he could slip his apartment key into her palm. A deep kiss
sealed the deal. Lillie asked why he wasn't angry at the shift
change. "I had no choice. I'm the low man."

Dog tired

At the canine rescue's 10th Annual Fur Ball, a woman at my round table of eight showed me a photo of her basset hound, Lulu, then asked about my dog. "I don't have a dog," I said. Six mouths stopped chewing their salads. Lulu's owner pursed her lips. "May I ask why?" I defensively listed my other canine-supporting voluntary actions – donating paper products for kennel cleanings, buying fundraising chicken BBQ tickets, sponsoring its Paws For Claus Christmas bazaar. But when the court waited for the truth, I confessed. "I like to sleep in." Finding my answer acceptable, they chewed on.

See you at Central Booking, you pdf whore

Congratulations on weaseling your way into my Spam folder last night. First thing this morning, I reported your email to the police. They agreed that your promise to "make my work frictionless" was, in fact, a death threat, that you wish to forcibly end my life. Without friction, all molecules would simply let go, birth rates would plummet, movement would stop, relationships would end, seedlings would never burst through a thin layer of soil toward the sun. No friction? No life. No friction? No growth. No friction? No me. Do not reply; I cannot accept emails while in witness protection.

Generational perennials

Yes, I admit telling Great-Grandma Fay that the color of her peonies easily rivaled that of a fine merlot. But I deny ever asking my matriarchal octogenarian to dig up its root ball, wrap the cluster in wet napkins, and slide it into a yellow Rite Aid bag. The next morning, her soil-stained fingers took my hands into hers. "Plant them when you get home before they realize they've been moved. Do that, and you'll always have my June blooms." Her soft yet urgent smile cemented a tradition. Bleeding hearts followed the next year, pink lilies the year after that.

One two three one two three

I would tune the dial to Polka Today on Sunday mornings to catch Bobby Vinton's *Melody of Love* or Will Glahe's *Roll Out the Barrel*, songs my Grandma Sophie would hum while her hands mixed white globs of farmer's cheese with onions and butter. "Watch," she would say. "Fill. Fold. Seal." I can still smell perogies when I wrap myself in my granny-square afghan, the one she assembled from bits and pieces of leftover yarn strands she kept tucked beside her bed. When she crocheted, her fingers fluttered like bathing birds. "Loop. Under. Through. You try now. One. Two. Three."

Thirty-two Septembers

After 3,200 high school students,
103,680 classroom bells,
401 college recommendation letters,
320 fire drills,
128 quarters
99 snow days,
96 very important trainings,
27 June graduations,
26 different English courses,
25 years of marriage,
16 bouts of stomach flu,
12,000 graded essays,
11 sparkly new principals,
10 student funerals,
9 Homecoming wins,
8 student teachers,
7 coffee pots,
6 deleted resignation letters,
5 different school districts,
4 fender benders in the school parking lot,
3 legit lockdowns,
2 epic cafeteria fights, and
1 file folder stuffed with thank you notes,
I drove home and didn't need to go back.

Poetry

Linger

On this warm evening, we chose to digest dinner
by meandering along the worn paths in our own backwoods,
the place where we once played hide and seek,
ignoring your mom's calls and my dad's threats,
all for just a little more us.

We walk the trails with entwined fingers,
outstretching our arms like strands of sweet taffy
over stumps and divots and marshy spots,
laughing as we recall the time this happened
and the time that happened.

On the back porch, we settle into our respective chairs
waiting for The Ursas to show themselves,
both as distant from us as our own thoughts of going inside.
As you brush your thumb over my knuckles,
I know we'll stay until the mosquitoes come for our ankles.

All books twenty-five cents

If I hadn't received silver coins
as change from my $3.10 ice coffee,
I wouldn't have found
the book about novel writing
wedged in a bin at my local bookstore's
Summer Sidewalk Sale.

In The Writer's Digest's Handbook:
How to Write a Novel, writing teacher
Gary Provost's simple sentence on page 141
clarified, cemented the goal:
novelists should not write for readers
to finish the book, but to turn the page.

Like life, we don't live for endings.
We live for what's next —
a voice, a scent, a song
a giggle, a touch, a kiss
a day.

We turn our own pages.
Others turn ours.
We turn others'.

For that sterling lesson,
I paid a quarter.

The poetry student's question

How do you know
when a poem holds the stamina
to stand upright against a wind gust
strong enough to topple its letters
into a jagged pile of nothing?

On good days, the poet simply fans
orange embers into warm verse.
On most days, poets must force and drag,
leaving poet and poem badly bruised,
unfit and unready for public viewings.

It's the poets' vow,
the teacher said,
to couple what they already know
with what they have yet to understand
until life or death do them part.

.

The poetry criminals

Poets are criminals by default.
They basically engage in a glorified game
of Ding Dong Ditch by planting ticking time bombs
onto unsuspecting synapses before
turning and running for their own lives.
Their crime?
Inflicting forcible introspection onto innocent victims
who were just out for a good read.

(And!) These poets, these villains, are allowed to do this
as often as they wish to whomever they please
without a license
without a background check
without a mandatory waiting period
even without having at least one statement
certifying their good moral character.
Jeez Louise.

Guiltless, these misfits limp on
knowing their words have the power
to bump a life back on course,
to push a straining soul to a summit,
to give a mind exactly what it didn't know it needed –
enough time to spot a dark storm advancing from the west
or to witness blond strands unfold over the eastern horizon
in a morning's purple mist.

Eagle cam addict

High in an evergreen overlooking Big Bear Lake
two celebrity bald eagles warm their eggs
in a half-ton nest of woven branches and sticks.

I was one of the tens of thousands who watched
and waited to see the first pip, the spot an eaglet
breaks through the eggshell with its eyetooth.

Its live chat fed a hungry viewing audience,
all lost in wonder about what-ifs and what-nots.
All for us, from sunrise to moonrise to sunrise again.

More than once, I suppressed my Truman Show desire
to belt out "Good morning, and in case I don't see ya,
good afternoon, good evening, and good night."

But I'm left to wonder if I'm no better than a voyeur
who looks just because she can, never even thinking
to ask Jackie and Shadow for permission to peep.

.

When lawnmowers fall silent on a summer day

I hear a cardinal's what-cheer what-cheer
a blue jay's queedle queedle
a mourning dove's double coos
a house wren's trilly trills
a robin's tuts and whinnies
a goldfinch's crisp chirps
a chickadee's two-toned feeee-bee
a bluebird's low tu-a-wee
until the next mowing.

Reply letter from my nephew

thank you for the stamps /
they're real expensive at the PX
I can't have food or books or pictures
that are even // slightly inappropriate //
For some reason others walk around
like it's hell or something / but it's the same
as high school as far as the types of people go
/ there's kids who mess around the whole time /
kids who are suckups / everything like that /
the ones that make me mad are the ones
who try to shortcut // everything //
and that's what gets us in the most trouble /
It's sort of like prison / but I enjoy it /
I fell asleep during my watch / just once /
Thank you for writing to me, Aunt Catherine,
// I can read your cursive just fine //
Not everyone gets a letter.

You tell me

Does spilling coffee
on my white pants during my commute
simply prove I'm an absolute klutz
or does it signify that it's time to revise my resume
to find a job that gives my life some actual meaning?

Is following a dim trail
through a swamp on a rainy afternoon
the perfect setting for a nature poem
or more of a metaphor for the radiologist unable
to find a heartbeat in my abdomen at thirty-two weeks?

Just tell me, already.
How deeply should I read? Set a limit.
Do I look inward with a microscope
or upward with a telescope or outward, backward,
forward, seaward and homeward, all at the same time?

Inching

Me: We did it.
You: It's all ours.

Me: I never thought it would actually happen.
You: Same.

Me: I packed a bottle of champagne in the car. I'll grab it.
You: Let's measure first.

Me: My God. I forgot the tape measure.
You: You did not.

Me: I did.
You: But I reminded you.

Me: Yes. I remember.
You: You said, "Thanks for reminding me. I'll grab it now."

Me: Yes, I remember that, too.
You: I still think you're kidding.

Me: When I went into the kitchen, I was thirsty. After a glass,
I never went back.
You: We drove here tonight to see if it would fit.

Me: I'm sure it will.
You: We're not moving it here only to find it doesn't.

Me: Then we have to wait.
You:

You: What else can we do here now?
Me: Start cleaning, I suppose.

You: I'll get the champagne.
Me: For good measure.

Drama: One-Act Play

Internal Suspension: A One-Act Play

A high school principal's day goes from bad to worse when his disciplinary decisions backfire leaving permanent consequences in their wake.

Cast

Mitch Walker, a high school principal in his 40s
Caroline Callahan, a businesswoman in her 40s
Ayden Walker, a 16-year-old high school student
Melody Harper, a 22-year-old college student

Act 1, Scene 1: A high school principal's office, day.

An office door is open wide enough to display a nameplate that reads MITCH WALKER, HIGH SCHOOL PRINCIPAL. Three chairs, enough to hold a set of parents and a student in need of discipline, face the principal's desk. An easel holds a HOME OF THE BOMBERS placard in blue and orange lettering. A wall calendar reads DECEMBER.

A lone window shows falling snow. It separates a short couch from tall, wide bookshelves loaded with sports memorabilia -- three footballs on wooden holders, a #7 football jersey with the name WALKER on the back, several trophies, and two large motivational prints with clear messages: "There Is No I in Team" and "Your Attitude Determines Your Direction". On a middle shelf sits two framed photos -- one of a graying man with a blond clinking champagne glasses, the other of a non-smiling teenager. Two not-yet distinguishable items are also on the shelf -- a narrow strip of paper and a small pile of colored string.

At the far end of his office, a table holds a football secured within a clear display case; a golden lamp attached to the wall shines down on it, illuminating it like a shrine.

Stocky-framed and graying MITCH WALKER stomps into his office carrying two pink sheets of paper clutched in one hand and a full bottle of whiskey in the other. He wears brown loafers, tan slacks, a blue long-sleeved dress shirt, and a blue and orange striped tie. The lanyard around his neck holds his plastic school ID.

Mitch kicks the door shut behind him, almost tripping over a small garbage can beside his desk. He sets the whiskey bottle beside his desk phone then reads the pink papers.

Still examining the pink pages, he moans while walking the length of his office to the football display case. He pauses to buff its corner. He turns back to his desk, then crumples up one of the pink papers and shoots it at his garbage can, but misses. The balled-up paper rests beside the can on the floor. He sets the other pink paper on his desk and plops himself into his desk chair.

MITCH: Suspended! The Superintendent wouldn't even listen.

Mitch plunks his elbows on his desk and drops his head into them. He does not notice CAROLINE CALLAHAN, a sleekly dressed woman, slip into his office. She closes the door. She wears a black pencil skirt, a white blouse buttoned to the top and a short black blazer that matches her black pumps. Her brown hair is pinned up in a tight bun.

CAROLINE: Hello, Mr. Walker.

MITCH: *(whirls toward the door)* Mrs. Callahan. You're here already.

Mitch stands, motioning to Caroline to sit in the first chair in front of his desk, but Caroline bypasses the chairs to first examine his bookshelves before taking a seat across from him.

CAROLINE: I take discipline matters regarding my son very seriously. I came right over.

Mitch sits. Caroline smooths her skirt.

MITCH: Of course. As do I.

The two sit facing each other in silence. Fidgety Mitch folds his hands on top of the pink paper. Relaxed Caroline crosses her legs. Caroline notices the bottle on his desk and cocks her head.

CAROLINE: Whiskey for breakfast, I see.

MITCH: *(snatches the whiskey bottle)* I just confiscated it out of a gym locker. Never a dull moment in a high school.

He tucks it inside a desk drawer.

CAROLINE: Ayden has never even had a detention before. Explain to me how he can be suspended. He's the president of the National Honor Society.

MITCH: *(leans back, sighs)* I know.

CAROLINE: *(with clear annunciation)* He has had perfect attendance since kin-der-gar-ten.

MITCH: I know.

CAROLINE: Tell me what the hell is going on.

MITCH: *(tries to read from the pink paper)* According to his Music teacher, he...

CAROLINE: *(interrupts, points at the bookshelves)* I noticed that nice picture you have over there.

Mitch stops reading.

MITCH: Oh. Um. Yeah. That was Missy's favorite photo from our trip over the summer.

Caroline stands and picks up the frame, examining the photo, then the frame more closely. She smiles, then taps the glass with her fingernail. She sits, propping the frame on her crossed knee.

CAROLINE: You and Missy both look happy. Look at those smiles. Lovely.

MITCH: Thank you. *(tries to read from the pink report)* I'd like to read...

CAROLINE: *(interrupts)* It's lovely that you chose to use the frame that once held our wedding photo for a new one with your new wife. *(Quite grittily)* So Mitch, did you remove ours or just shove the new one on top?

MITCH: Caroline.

CAROLINE: That frame was a wedding gift from my grandmother. I suppose I should have claimed it as my property in our divorce papers. *(Speaks more to herself)* I should file an appeal notice.

MITCH: I'll have the frame couriered to your office tomorrow. I suppose it is technically yours.

CAROLINE: Not technically. Absolutely. It is absolutely mine.

MITCH: Of course. *(hesitates, then decides to "go there")* Maybe you could send me the binder of my father's baseball cards. I left it on a shelf in the basement.

Caroline purses her lips then readjusts herself in the chair. She stares at the floor, exhales then looks at Mitch.

CAROLINE: Liam. He. He sold them.

Mitch blinks. He sits motionless for a few moments before lurching his torso forward in the chair, head facing down, as though punched in the stomach. His genuine grief is a surprise to both. He lifts his head to look at his ex-wife.

MITCH: You couldn't take the time to check with me? A quick call. A text.

CAROLINE: *(attempts sincerity)* Liam thought it was best.

MITCH: *(mimics her)* Liam thought it was best.

CAROLINE: *(stands holding the frame)* He did it three years ago after we separated, when Ayden was a freshman. Liam put the money into a CD in Ayden's name. I found it to be a thoughtful gesture.

MITCH: *(goes to her)* You really dropped the ball, Caroline. You had no right!

Mitch grabs the picture frame and smashes it on the floor. Broken wood and shattered glass rest at their feet. Caroline screams. She falls to her knees and picks up wooden pieces.

CAROLINE: How could you do such a thing?

MITCH: Easy. I just had to stoop to your level, to Liam's level.

Caroline stands. She walks to the football display case and runs her finger along the top. She doesn't look at him; she talks to the case.

CAROLINE: You treated me more like a teammate than a wife. That's what ended our marriage.

MITCH: You're the one who filed the papers.

CAROLINE: I was tired of having you there but not there. You were stuck somehow, trapped in the past, I suppose. *(She taps the protective case.)* This means more to you than our marriage ever did.

MITCH: That's ridiculous, and I wasn't trapped in the past.

CAROLINE: Really?

She lifts the football display case, turns to Mitch.

MITCH: Put that down.

She raises the case to shoulder height.

CAROLINE: If I drop this right now, your precious football might get scratched with glass. Punctured even. *(She gives a fake gasp then lowers the case.)* Listen to me, Mitch. Our son is a musical prodigy. Ayden cannot be suspended. He is destined to attend the best schools and play with some of the best musicians in the world.

MITCH: You never gave him a chance to like football.

CAROLINE: He likes the piano. He's good at the piano.

Mitch takes the case from Caroline and sets it back on the table. He polishes a corner with his elbow.

MITCH: He could have been the quarterback if he had just started when he was younger like I had wanted.

CAROLINE: So it's my fault I didn't force him to play contact sports. Unbelievable. In addition to being a top football coach, you've become an expert in the blame game.

Mitch points at the falling snow.

MITCH: A prodigy, huh? It would be a cold day in hell before you ever allowed him to explore his own interests.

CAROLINE: You mean your interests. You know what our son is? Happy. He's not some disgruntled teenager. Ayden has good grades; he talks to me.

A soft "hmpf" escapes Mitch's lips, ending the conversation. He sits at his desk and picks up the pink paper. Caroline goes to the window to watch the snow.

MITCH: I have to address what happened with Ayden here at the high school.

CAROLINE: *(remains at window, listens)* Fine. Proceed.

Mitch was about to read when AYDEN WALKER runs in. He wears black joggers and a gray sweatshirt. His hair is pulled back into a man-bun. Ignoring his mother's presence, he points an accusatory finger at his father's face.

AYDEN: Melody was just removed as a student teacher! She won't be able to graduate next week. Who the hell do you think you are?

MITCH: It's more complicated than that and you know it.

AYDEN: Because you are making it more complicated. *(He goes to Caroline by the window, hugs her)* Mom! You have to fix this.

Caroline guides Ayden to the chairs facing Mitch. Both sit.

CAROLINE: Mitch. Tell me what is going on.

MITCH: *(reads the pink paper)* The music teacher learned that her student teacher and Ayden have been, well, texting each other. She chose to go over my head and report her suspicions directly to the Superintendent's office. An investigation was launched into the electronic communications between Miss Harper and our son. Ayden has been suspended pending a disciplinary hearing and Miss Harper has been removed from the student teaching program. The actual report of their communication has not been shared with me due to an obvious conflict of interest.

CAROLINE: *(whispers to Ayden)* Oh my God. Were you sexting?

AYDEN: Mom! You have to believe me. Nothing happened! We talked. We texted. That's it. Dad - You have to believe me.

All three fall silent. Mitch and Caroline look at each other and then at Ayden.

CAROLINE: Ayden, what is the report going to say?

AYDEN: Mom! Melody is twenty-two. I'm almost seventeen. We're practically adults.

CAROLINE: *(to herself)* A music teacher named Melody.

MITCH: Well, in New York State, son, that's a Class E felony.

AYDEN: We love each other!

MITCH: Tell us what the investigation is going to reveal.

Ayden refuses to speak. Caroline puts her hand on her chest, agonizing at a revelation.

CAROLINE: Your state recital is next weekend. *(becoming unhinged)* Damn it! Tell us what you did!

AYDEN: I fell in love. Is that so wrong?

CAROLINE: You're sixteen years old.

Ayden marches to the shelves, snatches up a strip of photos.

AYDEN: Look at these photos. There has to be a reason you kept this, Dad. We were a real family back then. Remember how we all crammed into the photo booth at the Grand Canyon during that summer trip?

Mitch takes the photos. Mitch and Caroline examine them.

MITCH: Our last family vacation before...

CAROLINE: Look at our smiles.

MITCH: That's why I keep it here. I always want to remember that moment.

Ayden takes another item from the shelves. He holds up a string bracelet.

AYDEN: I remember this, too.

CAROLINE: We must have made a hundred friendship bracelets between New York and Arizona on that road trip.

AYDEN: We all liked each other back then. I want to make those kinds of memories with Melody. Mom. Dad. Melody is my soulmate. Just because the two of you gave up on love doesn't mean that I should.

Mitch and Caroline take a jolted step back.

MITCH: I understand that you think you love Melody.

CAROLINE: And that you also knowingly and appropriately love the piano.

The photo strip Mitch had been holding slips from his hand to the floor.

MITCH: I understand that you are a fancy musical genius, but I never realized until right now that you are nothing more than a clueless, immature fool.

Ayden throws his hands up into the air and storms over to the encased football.

CAROLINE: My God, Mitch, you've lost your mind.

MITCH: I can assure you that a lack of love had absolutely nothing to do with our divorce.

In unison, AYDEN: Really?   CAROLINE: Really?

MITCH: Yes, really!

In runs MELODY HARPER, a brainy, young brunette wearing glasses, white canvas sneakers, cropped jeans and a sweatshirt that reads "The Best Players Are On The Bench" over piano keys.

MELODY: Ayden!

AYDEN: Melody!

Melody and Ayden kiss. Caroline goes to Mitch's side.

MELODY: *(to Ayden)* I heard you were suspended because of me.

AYDEN: *(to Melody)* It's okay. My dad is going to fix everything.

MELODY: Can you do that, Mr. Walker?

In unison, MITCH: No.   CAROLINE: Yes.

CAROLINE: *(confidently)* He will fix this. *(To Mitch)* We are talking about our son here. You have to act. For once, Mitch, engage in his life. Put him first.

Mitch loosens his tie then waves his arm to show a large area.

MITCH: None of you understand the enormity of the situation. *(to Ayden and Melody)* We're not talking about a few innocent texts. Are we?

Ayden and Melody stare at their shoes.

CAROLINE: *(pleads to Mitch)* Go to the Superintendent. Explain they are young and foolish. Think about it -- you can actually be the defense to your son's offense.

MELODY: Oh, I love sports metaphors.

Mitch's ego is triggered. He walks over to the table holding his prized football, picks up the case and walks toward his desk. He stops in the center of his office. Caroline spots the strip of pictures on the floor, picks it up, and props it on the windowsill.

MITCH: *(to Ayden and Melody)* Neither of you deserve it, but I'll try talking to him again.

MELODY: Oh, thank you, Mr. Walker. Thank you for giving

me a chance. *(She points at a poster on the shelf.)* There really is no I in TEAM.

AYDEN: Thanks for believing in me, Dad.

Ayden gives Melody the friendship bracelet; she slides it onto her wrist as though she is sliding on an engagement ring. Melody squeals in delight. She claps her hands together and hops up and down. All turn to her.

MELODY: I wasn't going to say anything until later, but I feel like this is a true family moment. *(a beat)* I'm pregnant!

AYDEN: Mom! Dad! I'm going to be a dad!

Melody jumps into Ayden's arms. Mitch drops his treasured box, which breaks into several pieces. Caroline faints.

Act 1, Scene 2: A high school principal's office, evening

Six inches of snow now rest on the outside windowsill. The "Your Attitude Determines Your Direction" poster is vertically torn in two and now covers the HOME OF THE BOMBERS placard.

The wooden table that had once held a prized football now sits at center stage holding a half-empty bottle of whiskey. Mitch's tie hangs over a corner. The short couch has been pulled up behind it.

Mitch and Caroline sit slumped side by side on the couch. The two top buttons of Mitch's shirt are undone. He now wears his old football jersey that he managed to pull over his dress shirt. A glass of whiskey rests loosely in his hand. Caroline's tight bun has loosened and looks a mess; her blazer is balled up behind her head as a makeshift pillow. She balances her whiskey glass on her knee. When they speak, their voices are hollow.

MITCH: I'm going to lose my job.

CAROLINE: He's going to miss the recital.

Remaining entirely still, they each move only an arm to raise the glasses of whiskey to their lips for a long sip.

Mitch's desk phone rings. Still holding his glass, he sits behind the desk and answers the call. He stares at the ceiling.

MITCH: Yes. Of course. I understand. I'll be in your office first thing in the morning. *(He hangs up.)*

CAROLINE: How bad is it?

MITCH: Melody, er, Miss Harper, just posted her sonogram pictures to Instagram.

Again, they move just enough to take long sips from their glasses.

CAROLINE: You've led the football team to three consecutive state titles. You won't lose your job. You're untouchable.

Mitch shakes his head. He goes to the shattered case and picks up the football. He checks its firmness.

MITCH: Come on. Go long.

Caroline sets her drink on the table. The two go to opposite sides of his office. Mitch throws her a solid spiral.

CAROLINE: You said we never stopped loving each other. *(throws football to Mitch)*

MITCH: That's right. We just stopped liking each other. *(throws football to Caroline)*

CAROLINE: *(rests football on her hip)* We will make public peace for the benefit of our grandchild. That is a non-negotiable. Do you understand? *(throws football to Mitch)*

MITCH: *(nods)* I wasn't stuck in the past like you said earlier. I was just stuck.

CAROLINE: You never trusted me enough to share that. I was your wife.

MITCH: *(exhales the air from his lungs)* And now I have Missy.

Mitch hands the football to Caroline, then drags the couch back to the wall and moves the empty bottle and glasses to his desk.

Caroline notices the crumpled pink paper beside the garbage can. She tucks the football under her elbow, picks up the balled-up paper, and smooths it out. She reads to herself.

CAROLINE: My God. You knew. You knew about them.

Mitch turns to see Caroline reading from the page he thought he had thrown away.

MITCH: *(sighs, nods)* I knew.

CAROLINE: Mitch, you knew months ago. And you did nothing? You didn't tell me. You didn't stop it.

Mitch moves under the light that once lit up his treasured football case.

MITCH: It's all there in black and white, isn't it? Back in October, a science teacher reported her suspicions to me but Ayden and Melody both denied it. Said I was nuts, that I was overreacting. Then two chaperones thought they spotted them getting hot and heavy under the bleachers at the Homecoming dance. I didn't write them up. I issued no disciplinary consequences for either of them. *(His anger grows.)* When the music teacher insisted there was a relationship between the two at a faculty meeting last week, do you know what I did? I laughed at her. Right there in front of everyone. I told her *she* was nuts, that *she* was the one overreacting. *(Yelling now.)* I mean the kid hasn't missed a day of school since kin-der-gar-ten, right? He's the God-damned president of the National Honor Society!

CAROLINE: *(realistically grim)* Other people saw them together. There are messages, texts, posts. Ayden will be marked a fool. He'll be dragged through the mud. So will Melody. And you.

MITCH: I took a gamble. I thought I could protect him.

Caroline turns the pink paper over and reads the back.

CAROLINE: *(gasps)* Mitch. This is about you. It's not just Ayden. You're being suspended, too.

MITCH: I can resign or be terminated at the next Board meeting. I followed my heart to the end of the Earth and fell over the edge.

Caroline grimaces at his comment, allowing the wrinkled pink paper to cascade to the floor.

CAROLINE: 'Tis nobler in the mind to suffer the slings and arrows of outrageous fortune or to take arms against a sea of troubles?

MITCH: Vince Lombardi?

CAROLINE: William Shakespeare. *(a beat)* Your inaction was your action. Again.

MITCH: *(goes to Caroline)* I can fix it. All of it.

Caroline sees him for who he will always be. She moves away from him and drops the football into the garbage can.

CAROLINE: Look who dropped the ball now.

She leaves.

Mitch goes to the window, takes the strip of photos and heads for the door. He stops short at the garbage can, reaches in, and lifts out the football. He holds the photos in his right hand and the football in his left. He looks between the two items, mentally determining their worth. He drops the photos into the garbage can, tucks the football under his elbow, and walks out the door.

THE END

Internal Suspension Discussion Questions

1) Mitch and Caroline have several disagreements. Would you classify those arguments as deep or trivial? Why?

2) What rings true or false about Mitch and Caroline being a divorced couple?

3) While Mitch, Caroline, Ayden and Melody share little to no humor with each other, what plot elements would the audience find funny and why?

4) Which moments of the story were emotionally touching?

5) Reread Ayden's comments just before Melody arrives at the principal's office. How is he an effective manipulator?

6) What caused Mitch's downfall?

7) What will likely happen to each of the characters within a year?

8) The phrase "internal suspension" is a common punishment given to students for unruly or inappropriate behavior. How does the play's title serve as a metaphor for each member of the family?

ABOUT THE AUTHOR

Catherine D'Agostino worked as a journalist for small-town newspapers before beginning a 32-year career teaching writing and literature to high school and college students in western New York. Readers ranked her mystery novel, *Braided Lies: A Thousand Islands Castle Mystery*, a five-star mystery. She is a member of the Friends of Chautauqua Writers' Center and lives in Fredonia, NY.

To schedule an in-person or virtual author visit to a book club, library, classroom, or community group, send an email to ironpelicanpublications@gmail.com.

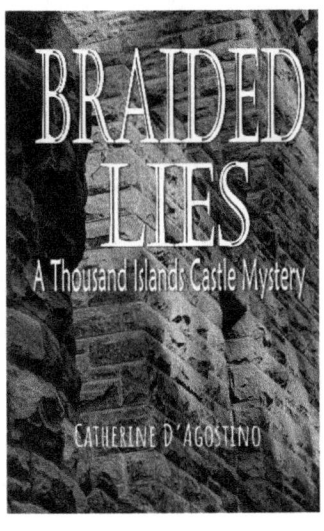